THE OFFICIAL
EVERTON FC
ANNUAL 2019

Written by Darren Griffiths
Designed by Chris Dalrymple

A Grange Publication

© 2018. Published by Grange Communications Ltd., Edinburgh,
under licence from Everton Football Club. Printed in the EU.

ISBN: 978-1-912595-08-2

CONTENTS

THE MARCO SILVA STORY... SO FAR

Marco Alexandre Saraiva da Silva, to give him his full name, was born in the Portuguese capital city of Lisbon on 12 July 1977.

As a player he was a right-back who played for a variety of Portuguese clubs, mainly in the second and third divisions, finishing his career with a six-year spell at Estoril. He retired from playing in June 2011 and was immediately appointed as Estoril's Director of Football. However, early into the season, he was named as the team manager. He did brilliantly well and only lost four times in 25 matches to help Estoril return to the top division as champions. Not surprisingly, Silva was ultimately chosen as the league's Manager of the Year.

Estoril then did better than anyone imagined in the Portuguese Premier League (Primeira Liga), finishing fifth in the table in 2012 to secure qualification to the UEFA Europa League. The team played great football and Silva's talent as a coach didn't go unnoticed by the bigger clubs in Portugal. He was appointed as the new manager of Sporting in May 2014. He led the team to third place in the table in 2015 and they also won the Portuguese Cup (the Taça de Portugal) by beating SC Braga 3-1 on penalties in the final after a 2-2 draw. Braga were actually winning 2-0 with just six minutes remaining but Sliva's team hit back in dramatic fashion! They had beaten Portuguese giants FC Porto on the way to the final.

In July 2015, Silva was named as the new manager of Greek outfit Olympiakos, whom he subsequently guided to a record–breaking 17 consecutive league wins from the first match of the season. During that run they also won 3-2 at the Emirates Stadium against Arsenal in the European Champions League group stage. Silva's team were by far the best in Greece and they won the 2016 title with six games remaining. They finished an astonishing THIRTY points ahead of second–placed Panathinaikos!

In January 2017, Silva decided to try his luck in the Premier League and was announced as head coach of Hull City when Mike Phelan was dismissed with the team rock–bottom of the Premier League. Under Silva, the Tigers fought back and recorded wins against Manchester United (in the EFL Cup) and Liverpool in the Premier League (Oumar Niasse scoring in both games) but they just failed to avoid the drop.

After the team's relegation, Silva resigned but in May 2017 it was confirmed that he would remain in the Premier League with Watford. He stayed at Vicarage Road until January 2018.

He started as the manager of Everton in June 2018, saying:

> "I am in a big, big Club and I think we can build a fantastic relationship and give our fans what they expect because they expect results. Of course, I have my own idea of what I will bring for Everton but I will respect the culture of the Club, the Everton culture. You cannot take away the ambition from our fans. This pressure is normal in a big club. We want this pressure behind us. It is not only about winning, they want to come and enjoy what they see. You need to deliver all these good feelings for them."

20 THINGS YOU DIDN'T KNOW ABOUT THEO WALCOTT

1. Theo was born in Stanmore, London on 16 March 1989. Little Britain star Matt Lucas was also born there; so was rock star Billy Idol.

2. In September 2004, Theo came off the bench to become the youngest player to play in the Southampton reserve team, at 15 years and 175 days.

3. In 2005, he played for Southampton in the FA Youth Cup final. They lost to Ipswich Town and on the Saints bench was Gareth Bale!

4. At the start of the following season, in the Championship, he became the youngest-ever Southampton first team player, at 16 years and 143 days.

5. Amazingly, before his first season at Southampton was over, he signed for Arsenal in January 2006.

6. Before he could make his senior debut for the Gunners, Theo was named in Sven Goran Eriksson's England squad for the 2006 World Cup.

7. On 30 May 2006, he became England's youngest-ever senior player by appearing in a 3-1 friendly win over Hungary at Old Trafford, aged 17 years and 75 days.

8. Theo was voted as the BBC Young Personality of the Year for 2006, four years after Wayne Rooney won it.

9. His first goal for Arsenal came in the 2007 League Cup final against Chelsea.

10. In April 2008, he was a torchbearer for the Olympic Flame for Beijing 2008 as it was paraded around London.

11. In 2008 he took over the number 14 jersey at Arsenal that had been worn by Thierry Henry.

12. On 10 September 2008 he became the youngest player in history to score a hat-trick for England, having been selected in the team ahead of David Beckham

13. In June 2009 he played for England in the final of the European Under-21 Championships. Stuart Pearce's team lost 4-0 to a Germany side that included Manuel Neuer and Mezut Ozil.

14. David Yates, the partner of Theo's aunty Yvonne, directed the Harry Potter movies and Theo nearly made a guest appearance in one of them but was too busy with his football!

15. Theo writes children's story books and has had four published so far.

16. In December 2012 he scored three and provided two assists as Arsenal beat Newcastle 7-3 - one of his goals won the BBC Goal of the Month competition

17. He scored the opening goal of the 2015 FA Cup final, with Arsenal eventually thrashing Aston Villa 4-0.

18. He was an unused substitute when Arsenal won the 2017 FA Cup final against Chelsea.

19. On 17 January 2018, Theo signed for Everton.

20. His first goals for the Toffees came in a 2-1 win against Leicester City at Goodison Park.

HOW MUCH DO YOU KNOW ABOUT... EVERTON!?

Try this fantastic bumper quiz and see if you know more about your favourite team than any of your friends...

The Stadium

1. In what year was Goodison Park built?

_____

2. What stand is opposite the Main Stand?

_____

3. Is the record attendance,
   a) 88,299 **b)** 78,299 or **c)** 68,299?

_____

4. True or False - Goodison Park is the only club stadium in Britain to ever host a World Cup semi-final?

_____

Goals!

1. Who scored Everton's last goal of last season?

_____

2. What is Dixie Dean's record-breaking tally of league goals in one season?

_____

3. Who was Everton's top scorer last season?

_____

4. Everton's record Premier League win was achieved against both Southampton and Sunderland - was it **a)** 6-0; **b)** 7-0 or **c)** 7-1?

_____

Players

1. Before joining Everton, Gylfi Sigurdsson played in the Premier League for two other teams - can you name them both?

_____

2. Which three Everton players appeared in the World Cup this summer?

_____

3. Which Everton player plays his international football for Columbia?

_____

4. Which two current Blues players joined the club from Sheffield United?

_____

Leighton Baines

1. From which club did Everton sign him?

_____

2. His only England goal came in 2012 in a win against **a)** Italy, **b)** Moldova or **c)** Estonia?

_____

3. How many England caps did he win - 25 or 30?

_____

4. In 2010–11 he won the Everton Goal of the Season award for a free–kick in the last minute of extra–time against which London team in the FA Cup?

_____

The FA Cup

1. Who did we beat in the 1995 FA Cup final?

_____

2. How many times have Everton won the FA Cup?

_____

3. In what year did Everton last reach the final - 2008 or 2009?

_____

4. Only one player has ever won two FA Cup finals with Everton. Is it **a)** Neville Southall, **b)** Dixie Dean or **c)** Dave Watson?

_____

Answers on p60.

PLAYER PROFILES (PART 1)

JORDAN PICKFORD #1

Goalkeeper
Signed: from Sunderland in 2018.
Best Everton moment: Saving a penalty against Hajduk Split in the Europa League in August 2017.

MASON HOLGATE #2

Defender
Signed: from Barnsley in 2015.
Best Everton moment: Making his first team debut against Tottenham at Goodison on the opening day of the 2016/17 season.

LEIGHTON BAINES #3

Defender
Signed: from Wigan Athletic in 2007.
Best Everton moment: Scoring a free-kick at Chelsea in the last minute of extra-time in the FA Cup in February 2011.

MICHAEL KEANE #4

Defender
Signed: from Burnley in 2018.
Best Everton moment: Opening the scoring against Hadjuk Split at Goodison Park in the Europa League in August 2017.

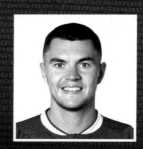

KURT ZOUMA #5

Defender
Signed: on loan from Chelsea in 2018.
Best moment in football: Playing in midfield when Chelsea won the League Cup final at Wembley in 2015.

PHIL JAGIELKA #6

Defender
Signed: from Sheffield United in 2007.
Best Everton moment: Scoring the winning penalty in the 2009 FA Cup semi–final shoot–out at Wembley against Manchester United.

ANDRE GOMES #8

Midfielder
Signed: on loan from Barcelona in 2018.
Best moment in football: Being a part of the Portugal squad that won the 2016 European Championship.

GYLFI SIGURDSSON #10

Midfielder
Signed: from Swansea City in 2017.
Best Everton moment: Scoring from 50 yards against Hajduk Split in the Europa League.

THEO WALCOTT #11

Winger
Signed: from Arsenal in 2018.
Best Everton moment: Scoring twice against Leicester City at Goodison in January 2018 to win the game 2–1.

MEET THE STAFF

ASSISTANT MANAGER: JOÃO PEDRO SOUSA

João Pedro Sousa first linked up with Marco Silva at Estoril and the pair's successful partnership has seen them go on to work together at Sporting Lisbon, Olympiakos, Hull City and Watford.

Sousa and Silva's relationship goes back to 1998, when they played together at Portuguese side Trofense.

Sousa's coaching career began as Under–19 coach at Braga.

Together, the pair won the Portuguese 2nd Division title with Estoril, before leading the club into European football for the first time after securing successive fifth and fourth–place finishes in the Primeira Liga.

They have also won the Portuguese Cup with Sporting Lisbon and secured a runaway Greek title success at Olympiakos.

FIRST TEAM COACH: DUNCAN FERGUSON

Club legend, Duncan Ferguson first came to Everton as a player from Glasgow Rangers in 1994. He quickly became a fans favourite, scoring his first goal in a Merseyside derby against Liverpool! He had a brief spell at Newcastle United but his heart has always been at Goodison and he returned to the club in 2000.

After retirement, he had a spell out of the game but returned to Everton again, this time as an Academy coach. He was appointed first team coach in 2014.

GOALKEEPING COACH: HUGO OLIVEIRA

Hugo Oliveira had 15 years of experience in Portugal before coming to Everton.

He has worked for the Portuguese national team and the famous Benfica, whom he joined in 2011.

In his time at Benfica, he worked with international keepers such as Julio Cesar and Jan Oblak.

He moved from Benfica to work with Marco Silva at Hull City in 2017 and was also part of the Everton manager's backroom staff at Watford.

FITNESS COACH: GONCALO PEDRO

Gonçalo Pedro's career began in the youth set-ups at Benfica and Sporting Lisbon, before he took on senior roles at Portimonense and SC Braga.

He then moved to Saudi Arabia, where he worked with their national Olympic team and club side Al Ahli.

He returned to Portugal to join Marco Silva at Estoril and has remained a key part of the manager's backroom team ever since.

HEAD OF PERFORMANCE: BRUNO MENDES

Bruno Mendes joined Marco Silva's backroom team as Head of Performance in summer 2018.

Prior to arriving on Merseyside, the highly-experienced fitness expert had spent over a decade with homeland club Sporting Lisbon.

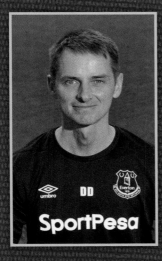

HEAD OF THERAPY SERVICES: DANNY DONACHIE

Danny was appointed Everton's Head of Therapy Services shortly after the arrival of Marco Silva in summer 2018.

The son of former Blues assistant manager Willie Donachie, Danny returned to the Club having previously been Head of Medicine prior to his departure in 2014.

Boasting years of experience working in top-level football, Donachie had served as Head of Medicine and Sports Science at Aston Villa before beginning his second spell with the Toffees.

DIRECTOR OF MEDICAL: DR ABOUL SHAHEIR

Dr Shaheir was appointed as Director of Medical at USM Finch Farm in October 2017.

He originally joined Everton in March 2015 as a club doctor. He started his career after graduating from medical school and was an orthopaedic surgeon for 13 years. He then became an accredited GP and has worked with both football and rugby clubs.

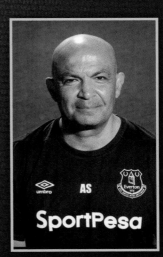

MY CAREER – by LUCAS DIGNE

Lucas Digne was born in France on 20 July 1993. He has played for some of the biggest clubs in Europe...and is now at the best! This is the Lucas Digne story so far...

1. I started my career with Lille in my home country of France, signing my first professional contract in July 2010 when I was 17 years old.

2. In July 2013 I signed for Paris St Germain.

3. In 2014 I played for France in the World Cup in Brazil. This is me against Ecuador. Antonio Valencia was sent off for this challenge.

4. In 2015 I played for PSG in the International Champions Cup in North America and Canada. We finished top after beating Benfica, Fiorentina and Manchester United.

5. In August 2015 I switched from France to Italy, joining Roma on a season–long loan.

6. I scored three goals for Roma, this is the very first one against FC Carpi.

7. I played against Real Madrid in the 2015–16 Champions League, marking Christiano Ronaldo!

8. I loved it at Roma but in July 2016 I was on the move again, this time to Barcelona!

9. This goal for Barcelona in the Champions League against Olympiakos was set–up for me by Lionel Messi.

10. Andres Iniesta is one of the best players I have ever played alongside.

11. Here's me training in Russia with the France squad during the World Cup. Sadly, I didn't play in any of the games but I was obviously delighted to be a part of it all.

12. I signed for Everton in the summer of 2018...

13. passed my medical...

14. ... and made my debut against Valencia in a friendly at Goodison Park.

SportPesa

DOMINIC CALVERT-LEWIN

CELEBRITY EVERTONIANS

How many of these celebrity Evertonians can you name...

1.

2.

3.

4.

5.

6.

7.

Here's your chance to fill up this page with photographs of Evertonians who you know! It could be family, friends, a teacher or even one of yourself! Paste the photo carefully into the box and write a line or two about them underneath.

Answers on p60.

EVERTON WORDSEARCH

See if you can find all the Everton-related words in the grid below.

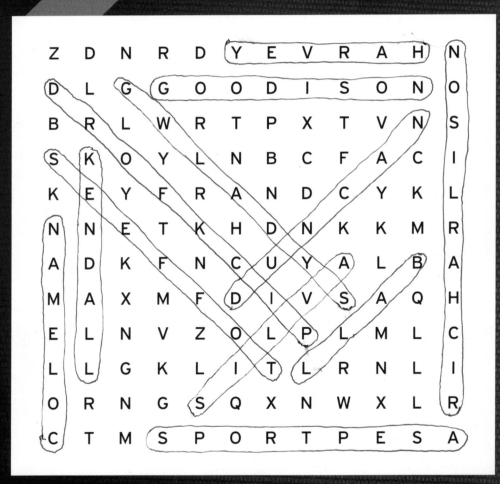

```
Z  D  N  R  D  Y  E  V  R  A  H  N
D  L  G  G  O  O  D  I  S  O  N  O
B  R  L  W  R  T  P  X  T  V  N  S
S  K  O  Y  L  N  B  C  F  A  C  I
K  E  Y  F  R  A  N  D  C  Y  K  L
N  N  E  T  K  H  D  N  K  K  M  R
A  D  K  F  N  C  U  Y  A  L  B  A
M  A  X  M  F  D  I  V  S  A  Q  H
E  L  N  V  Z  O  L  P  L  M  L  C
L  L  G  K  L  I  T  L  R  N  L  I
O  R  N  G  S  Q  X  N  W  X  L  R
C  T  M  S  P  O  R  T  P  E  S  A
```

Ball	Gwladys	Richarlison
Coleman	Harvey	Silva
Duncan	Kendall	SportPesa
Goodison	Pickford	Toffees

Answers on p60.

SEAMUS
COLEMAN

THE YERRY MINA STORY

Yerry Mina was born in Guachené, a town in the south west of Colombia with a population of just 20,000.

His first club was Deportivo Pasto, who he joined when he was 18. He made his senior debut at their home ground Estadio Libertad in March 2013 in the Copa Colombia, which is their version of the FA Cup.

Mina made his Categoría Primera A (Colombian Premier League) debut in September 2013.

His form caught the attention of Independiente Santa Fe, one of the most successful teams in Colombian history, and in December 2013 he joined them, initially on loan later becoming permanent.

He was a popular figure at Santa Fe and helped them to win a competition called the Superliga Colombiana in 2015. He scored one of the goals in the second leg of the final as Santa Fe defeated Atlético Nacional.

On 1 May 2016, Mina was on the move again when he signed for Brazilian side Palmeiras on a five-year contract. He was expected to represent Colombia at the 2016 Olympic Games in Rio de Janeiro but, sadly for him, he picked up an injury which ruled him out.

Without him, Colombia reached the quarter-finals but lost 2-0 against the hosts and eventual winners Brazil.

Mina fully recovered in August 2016, and played regularly during the latter part of the season, scoring vital goals to help Palmeiras win the Campeonato Brasileiro Série A (Brazilian Premier League) for the first time in 22 years. It was a ninth title win for Palmeiras, making them the most successful team in Brazil.

Mina was named in the Campeonato Brasileiro Série A 'Team of the Year'.

He was clearly doing exceptionally well in South America but wanted to test himself in Europe so in January 2018 he left Palmeiras and joined one of the biggest clubs in world football - Barcelona. In moving to the Nou Camp, he became the first Colombian ever to play for Barcelona.

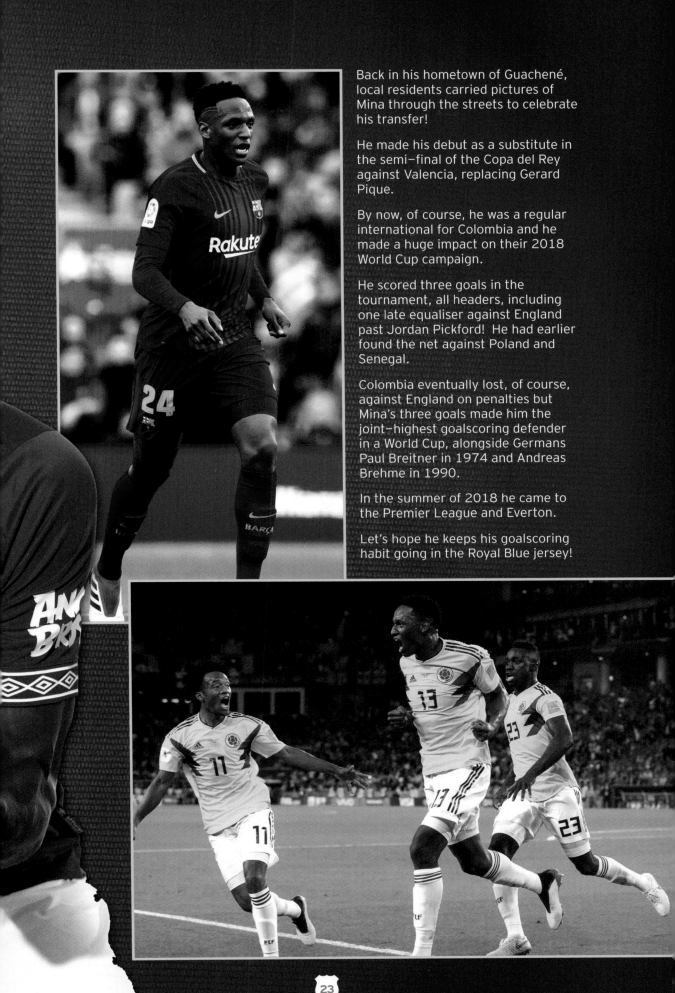

Back in his hometown of Guachené, local residents carried pictures of Mina through the streets to celebrate his transfer!

He made his debut as a substitute in the semi–final of the Copa del Rey against Valencia, replacing Gerard Pique.

By now, of course, he was a regular international for Colombia and he made a huge impact on their 2018 World Cup campaign.

He scored three goals in the tournament, all headers, including one late equaliser against England past Jordan Pickford! He had earlier found the net against Poland and Senegal.

Colombia eventually lost, of course, against England on penalties but Mina's three goals made him the joint–highest goalscoring defender in a World Cup, alongside Germans Paul Breitner in 1974 and Andreas Brehme in 1990.

In the summer of 2018 he came to the Premier League and Everton.

Let's hope he keeps his goalscoring habit going in the Royal Blue jersey!

NEW KIT PHOTO-SHOOT!

Every time a brand-new kit is launched, the players have to stop being footballers for a couple of hours and become fashion models instead!

Back in May 2018, this season's strip was revealed and a month earlier, Phil Jagielka and Jordan Pickford tried it on for size at a Goodison Park photo-shoot.

It's hard work for the players but, as you can see from our photographs, they also had a lot of fun!

DESIGN YO
OWN SHIRT

We are sure that you lo
new Everton kit – but wh
have a go at designing y
own. You can be as crea
you like and if you don't
to stick to the famous Ro
Blue and White jersey, th
design an away shirt. Tha
you can be as colourful a
like ; as long as it's not re

THE CENK TOSUN STORY

Cenk Tosun was born on 7 June 1991 in Wetzlar, Germany. His first professional club was Eintracht Frankfurt but he only ever made one appearance for the first team - he came off the bench against Wolfsburg in the Bundesliga in May 2010.

In January 2011 he signed for Turkish side Gaziantepspor and was an instant hit, scoring 10 goals in 14 games in his first season. Gaziantepspor is quite a new football club that was founded in 1969 and Tosun is third on their all-time goalscoring list with 51 goals. (Gaziantepspor have since fallen on hard times and have suffered consecutive relegations from the Super League to the third tier of Turkish football. They finished bottom of the second tier last season with just one point and a goal difference of minus 82! They actually accumulated ten points but had nine deducted for various reasons.)

After impressing with the club, Tosun switched to Beşiktaş in 2014 for half a million euros. He chose the number 23 jersey because of his fondness for the famous American basketball player Michael Jordan.

Tosun helped Beşiktaş win the Turkish Super League in his second and third seasons at the club. He was their top scorer in 2016/17 with 20 league goals - a tally that put him second in the Super League list for that season, three behind Brazilian Vagner Love and two ahead of former Everton striker Samuel Eto'o.

In 2017/18, Tosun scored four goals in six games as Beşiktaş won a tough UEFA Champions League group containing RB Leipzig, Monaco and Porto.

In January 2018 he joined Everton and made his debut at Wembley in the Premier League game against Tottenham Hotspur. His goals and his skill made him an instant favourite with the Everton fans. On signing for the Blues, he had this to say: "It feels great to be an Everton player. I'm really happy to be here and happy that everything is done. I'm really excited to play for Everton. It is a great club with a big history and a big culture and I'm looking forward to showing the fans the kind of player I am."

> **"** I believe I can be a good player in the Premier League for Everton. The Premier League is a strong league, I know that, so my own physical strength will help me. Also, I can use both feet the same and I believe I am a good striker in the box. **"**

At international level, Tosun represented Germany at various youth age–groups and on his debut for the Under–21 team in October 2013 he scored a penalty against an England side that had midfielder Henri Lansbury in goal! The English coach, Stuart Pearce, had substituted goalie Scott Loach at half–time and his replacement Jason Steele was sent off after conceding the second–half penalty from which Tosun scored. Lansbury had to take over in goal and did well to keep the score down to 2–0!

Despite doing well for the Germans, Tosun then changed his allegiance to Turkey and made his senior international debut in October 2013 against Holland in a World Cup qualifier. Turkey's 2–0 defeat ended their hopes of reaching the 2014 World Cup.

Tosun was part of the Turkey squad that played at Euro 2016 and he wore the number 9 shirt. Turkey failed to reach the knockout stage of the tournament after finishing third behind Croatia and Spain.

PLAYER PROFILES (PART 2)

LUCAS DIGNE #12
Defender
Signed: from Barcelona in 2018.
Best Everton moment: His Premier League debut against Wolverhampton Wanderers at Molineux in August 2018.

YERRY MINA #13
Defender
Signed: from Barcelona in 2018.
Best moment in football: Scoring three goals for Colombia in the 2018 World Cup, including one against England.

CENK TOSUN #14
Striker
Signed: from Beşiktaş in 2018.
Best Everton moment: Scoring both goals at Stoke City in March 2018 to secure a 2–1 victory.

JAMES McCARTHY #16
Midfielder
Signed: from Wigan Athletic in 2013.
Best Everton moment: His very first goal for the club on the last day of the 2013/14 season at Hull City.

IDRISSA GUEYE #17

Midfielder
Signed: from Aston Villa in 2016.
Best Everton moment: A thumping goal to clinch a 2–0 win at Huddersfield Town in April 2018.

MORGAN SCHNEIDERLIN #18

Midfielder
Signed: from Manchester United in 2017.
Best Everton moment: His first goal for the club during a 3–0 win against West Brom in March 2017.

OUMAR NIASSE #19

Striker
Signed: from Lokomotiv Moscow in 2016.
Best Everton moment: Coming off the bench against Bournemouth in September 2017 and scoring two goals to win the game.

BERNARD #20

Midfielder
Signed: from Shaktar Donetsk in 2018.
Best moment in football: Being part of the Brazil squad that won the 2013 FIFA Federations Cup.

MAARTEN STEKELENBURG #22

Goalkeeper
Signed: from Southampton in 2016.
Best Everton moment: Saving two penalties at Manchester City in October 2016 from Sergio Aguero and Kevin de Bruyne.

EVERTON IN THE COMMUNITY

Everton Football Club has its own official charity called Everton in the Community that helps thousands of people from all over Merseyside every year.

A few nights a week, the charity runs a programme called Kicks which gives young people from all over Liverpool a safe place to play sports and keep them off the streets and out of trouble. The Safe Hands programme helps young adults who have been in trouble with the police get their lives back on track.

The charity doesn't just help children and teenagers; it helps ex–soldiers and young men and children who struggle with mental health problems and one of its newer programmes, Stand Together, helps older people who are experiencing loneliness.

This year the charity celebrated its 30th birthday and since 1988 has been helping people young and old, from many different backgrounds, in lots of ways including health, education and helping people into employment.

Everton even has its own Free School which is open to young people aged 14–19 and provides exciting learning opportunities in a fantastic new building which is just a goal–kick from Goodison Park.

Throughout the season, the first–team players visit lots of Everton in the Community programmes to find out more about the great work they do and to meet the people that the charity helps. Sometimes they get involved with

They have recently used the money to buy and decorate a house for young people to live in to keep them off the streets.

Well done Unsy and the boys!

Everton in the Community fundraises throughout the year to raise money to help them continue their impressive work and there are lots of different ways that fans can get involved to help. Some Blues have done a skydive, abseiled down Liverpool Cathedral or taken part in the annual EitC Golf Day whilst local schools have held sponsored silences and cake stalls to help the charity of their favourite club.

The work that Everton in the Community does is recognised by people all over the world and in the last five years they have received over 100 awards for its brilliant ground–breaking work in helping others.

Everton in the Community also has a number of high–profile ambassadors and patrons who work to raise awareness of the charity's work, including Britain's Got Talent judge Amanda Holden and award–winning actress Dame Judi Dench.

classroom or sports sessions and they spend time playing games with old people or presenting trophies to the players at the charity's annual Disability Awards Ceremony.

At Christmas time, the full squad visits sick children at Alder Hey Children's Hospital and delivers presents to help put smiles on the faces of the young patients and their families.

> "One of the highlights of my year is the Disabled Football Awards. To see the smiles on the faces of the players and to see the pride they feel at representing Everton Football Club is just brilliant."
> **SEAMUS COLEMAN**

This year, Everton Under–23 manager David Unsworth and his Premier League 2 winning squad fundraised over £230,000 to support homeless people sleeping on the streets of Merseyside and they even slept out at Goodison Park themselves on a freezing cold night in November to experience homelessness for themselves.

> "The work that Everton in the Community does is absolutely incredible. Myself and the lads love getting along and getting involved. It's great to see the changes that they are making to the lives of so many people."
> **PHIL JAGIELKA**

SPOT THE DIFFERENCE

Can you find the eight differences between these two pictures?

HOME, AWAY OR DRAW!?

Here is a fixture list of 'matches' between Everton players who have played for the club in the Premier League. The player who scored the most goals for the Toffees wins the match. All you have to work out is whether each one is a home win, an away win or a draw.

To give you a clue - in these 10 games there are five home wins, four away wins and one draw! Mark H for a home win, A for an away win or D for a draw.

Good luck!

	Home		Away	Result
1	Victor Anichebe	v	Steve Pienaar	
2	Marouane Fellaini	v	David Unsworth	
3	Louis Saha	v	Yakubu	
4	Tomasz Radzinski	v	Andy Johnson	
5	Kevin Campbell	v	Tim Cahill	
6	Tony Hibbert	v	Tim Howard	
7	Gerard Deulofeu	v	Samuel Eto'o	
8	Sylvain Distin	v	John Heitinga	
9	Thomas Gravesen	v	Arouna Kone	
10	James McFadden	v	Nikica Jelavic	

Answers on p61.

HISTORY LESSON - BLUES FINISH 4TH

Optimism was in very short supply around Goodison Park during the summer of 2004.

Everton had finished the previous season in dreadful form, finishing just one place above the relegation zone after winning just one of their last ten Premier League games - a run that included defeats in each of the last four.

On top of that, their talismanic, teenage superstar Wayne Rooney looked to be heading through the exit door, with the big guns homing in on his precocious talent. And anyway, Rooney had been injured during the 2004 European Championships and so he wasn't available for pre-season training or friendlies, regardless of where his future lay. At the end of August he left Everton for Manchester United.

The only two new faces added to David Moyes' squad were Marcus Bent, a journeyman signed from Ipswich Town and Tim Cahill from Millwall, a young Australian who had never played in the Premier League before.

The doom and gloom deepened on the first day of the season when Everton were brushed aside, 4–1, by Arsenal at Goodison.

The following week, Everton fell behind to an early goal at Crystal Palace and it already looked as though it was going to be a long and difficult struggle for survival.

But then, incredibly, things got better.

Thomas Gravesen scored twice and Bent got the other as Everton chalked up a desperately needed 3–1 victory.

Confidence began to flow through the players, as indicated by a hard–fought 0–0 draw at Manchester United and then a 1–0 win at Manchester City. Indeed, Everton didn't lose again until early October, by which time they were third in the Premier League table.

The experts declared that, despite this astonishingly good start, Everton wouldn't sustain their good form and that they would soon slip down the table.

But they were wrong.

Lee Carsley scored a famous winner against Liverpool at Goodison in December and Everton found themselves second in the table. Some Evertonians were even dreaming of a first title win since 1987!

Gravesen was the inspiration behind the success but when Real Madrid came calling during the January transfer window, nobody could blame him for swapping Goodison for the Bernabeu. To counter the Dane's departure, Moyes brought in the relatively unknown Spanish midfielder Mikel Arteta; and the team kept picking up results.

Leon Osman scored a 92nd minute winner against Portsmouth, Marcus Bent netted an equalizer in stoppage time at Southampton, Aston Villa were dismantled at Villa Park and, ten years after scoring the only goal against Manchester United, Duncan Ferguson did it again in April.

Big Dunc swooped to head home a Kevin Kilbane cross to keep the Toffees firmly in the driving seat in the race with Liverpool for that coveted fourth place.

On May 7th, David Weir and Tim Cahill scored the two goals that beat Newcastle United and the following day Liverpool lost at Arsenal.

Everton had done it!

The most amazing fourth placed, Champions League qualification slot had been achieved; and didn't the Blue half of the city celebrate!

GYLFI SIGURDSSON

CAN YOU TELL THE FUTURE?

By the time you start to read your fab 2019 Everton Annual, the 2018/19 season will already be under way. But there's still a long way to go and still a lot of football to be played. See if you can predict who will be the winners and losers this season...

COMPETITION	2017/18	2018/19
PREMIER LEAGUE	Manchester City	
RELEGATED FROM THE PREMIER LEAGUE	Swansea City, Stoke City, West Bromwich Albion	
CHAMPIONSHIP	Wolverhampton Wanderers	
PROMOTED TO THE PREMIER LEAGUE	Aston Villa	
LEAGUE ONE	Wigan Athletic	
LEAGUE TWO	Accrington Stanley	
NATIONAL LEAGUE	Macclesfield Town	
FA CUP	Chelsea	
LEAGUE CUP	Manchester City	
SCOTTISH PREMIER LEAGUE	Celtic	
CHAMPIONS LEAGUE	Real Madrid	
EUROPA LEAGUE	Atletico Madrid	
PL GOLDEN BOOT	Mo Salah	
EVERTON TOP SCORER	Wayne Rooney	
TOTAL SCORE		

JUNIOR BLUES...

We all know that Everton have the best fans in world football!

Blues are born, not manufactured, and here are just some of the many hundreds of photographs we received when we invited you to show your true colours!

WORLD CUP REVIEW

Everton's Jordan Pickford was one of the undoubted stars of the 2018 World Cup in Russia.

The Blues number one fought off competition from Stoke City's Jack Butland and Burnley's Nick Pope to be the starting goalkeeper for Gareth Southgate's team and he duly turned in some terrific displays as England confounded pre-tournament predictions by reaching the semi-finals.

FACT: Pickford became only the fifth Everton player to ever play in a World Cup semi-final after Ray Wilson (1966), Slaven Bilic (1998), Nuno Valente (2006) and John Heitinga (2010).

England were in Group G in Russia, playing their games in Volgograd, Niznhy Novgorod and Kaliningrad.

After a stoppage-time winner from captain Harry Kane against Tunisia got the Three Lions off to a positive start, Pickford was a virtual spectator in the next match as Panama were brushed aside 6-1.

That result meant certain qualification to the knockout phase so a 1-0 defeat to Roberto Martinez's Belgium in the last fixture of the group didn't really matter. In fact, it probably worked in England's favour as it meant that they avoided Brazil and France!

It was the last 16 match against Colombia in Moscow that really propelled Pickford to hero status. Once again it was Harry Kane who gave England the lead and that was preserved until stoppage time. Cruelly, the 93rd minute equaliser came after Pickford had made the save of the tournament, diving acrobatically to turn behind a thunderbolt effort from Mateus Uribe. From the resulting corner, Yerry Mina squeezed home a heart-breaking leveller and no further goals in extra-time took the contest to penalties.

England had never won a World Cup penalty shoot-out - but then they'd never had an Everton goalie between the sticks! Pickford was the hero, superbly saving Carlos Bacca's spot-kick allowing Eric Dier to fire home the winning penalty.

Against all the odds, England were into the quarter-finals with Sweden barring their way to the last four. Again, Pickford was outstanding, making three fabulous saves as Southgate's men won 2-0, earning himself the official Man of the Match in the process.

So, for the first time since 1990, and for only the third time ever, England found themselves in a World Cup semi-final and they got off to a terrific start against Croatia in Moscow when Tottenham defender Kieran Trippier curled home a wonderful direct free-kick after just five minutes.

Sadly for Pickford and England, that was as good as it got and the longer the game went on, the stronger Croatia became. Goals from Ivan Perisic and Mario Mandzukic ended the dream and broke English hearts.

After a gallant World Cup, football wasn't coming home; but Jordan Pickford returned a national hero!

Pickford wasn't the only Everton player on duty in Russia during the summer. Gylfi Sigurdsson and Idrissa Gueye represented Iceland and Senegal respectively.

Iceland were in a tough group alongside Argentina, Croatia and Nigeria but after doing so well in the 2016 European Championships, hopes were high. They drew 1–1 with Argentina in their first game but then lost to Nigeria and Croatia (a game in which Sigurdsson scored) to finish bottom of the group.

Idrissa Gueye was even more unlucky. He played in all three games as Senegal beat Poland, drew with Japan and then lost against Colombia. They finished with an identical points and goals record as Japan but were eliminated on the fair–play rule after picking up more yellow cards. A desperately sad way to go out of a World Cup.

2018 WORLD CUP QUIZ

1. As well as England, who were the other beaten semi–finalists?

    _____

2. Harry Kane won the Golden Boot by scoring how many goals?

    _____

3. Apart from Kane, who was the only Englishman to score more than one goal?

    _____

4. When England won the penalty shoot–out 4–3 against Colombia, who was the only man to miss his spot–kick?

    _____

5. Which nation knocked Brazil out?

    _____

6. "The previous World Cup record was six but in this tournament there were twelve." What are we talking about?

    _____

7. Where did Germany finish in their group?

    _____

8. Who was the manager who guided France to glory in the final?

    _____

Answers on p61.

PLAYER PROFILES (PART 3)

SEAMUS COLEMAN #23

Defender
Signed: from Sligo Rovers in 2009.
Best Everton moment: Scoring an 87th minute winner against Crystal Palace at Selhurst Park in January 2017.

TOM DAVIES #26

Midfielder
Came through the ranks.
Best Everton moment: His terrific goal during an incredible 4–0 win against Manchester City at Goodison in January 2017.

KIERAN DOWELL #28

Midfielder
Came through the ranks.
Best Everton moment: Scoring a long–range cracker in Tanzania in the summer of 2017 against Kenyan champions Gor Mahia.

DOMINIC CALVERT-LEWIN #29

Striker
Signed: from Sheffield United in 2016.
Best Everton moment: His first goal for the club after just nine minutes against Hull City at Goodison in March 2017.

RICHARLISON #30

Striker
Signed: from Watford in 2018
Best Everton moment: Scoring two goals on his debut against Wolves at Molineux in August 2018

ADEMOLA LOOKMAN #31

Winger
Signed: from Charlton Athletic in 2017.
Best Everton moment: Scoring the fourth goal on his debut when Everton thrashed Manchester City 4–0 in January 2017.

JOAO VIRGINIA #33

Goalkeeper
Signed: from Arsenal 2018.
Best Everton Moment: Signing for the club in the summer of 2018.

BENI BANINGIME #34

Midfielder
Came through the ranks.
Best Everton moment: His first-team debut against Chelsea at Stamford Bridge in October 2017.

JONJOE KENNY #43

Defender
Came through the ranks.
Best Everton moment: His senior debut against Norwich City in the Premier League on the final day of the 2015/16 campaign.

THEO WALCOTT

NAME THE KEEPER...

Here are ten Premier League goalkeepers... see how many of them you can name.

1.

2.

3.

4.

5.

6.

7.

8.

9.

10.

Answers on p61.

EVERTON LADIES

Angharad James is 24 years old and her journey to the Everton Ladies team has been a fascinating one with plenty of ups and downs...

When did it start to get serious for you?

When I was a little older, a mate of mine applied to attend a college linked to Arsenal. She asked me to apply so I could come with her, so I did but in the end I got through and she didn't! I was put on the standby list for a place, then a week before the first term was due to start, someone dropped out, so off I went. I ended up having three years of college in London.

That must have been tough, leaving home and all your friends?

I was 15 at the time and I was moving away from literally fields to the big city. It was a massive move and the first few weeks I would ring home every day crying my eyes out. But I stuck at it and had three of the best years of my life.

How did the move to Bristol come about?

Laura Harvey was manager of Arsenal at the time and she asked if I wanted to go out on loan. I was 17 and too young to break into the first team so I went to Bristol on loan but with the intention of playing for Arsenal long term. The loan turned into me leaving and I just stayed at Bristol. But it was the best thing for me because I would have struggled to break through at Arsenal but at 17, 18 I was starting in WSL1 for Bristol. I learned so much in my time there.

When did your football journey start, Angharad?

I used to play rugby – I am Welsh aren't I?! – but when I got to 11 or 12, I couldn't play with the boys anymore so I went to play for a girls' team but believe it or not I was too strong! I couldn't enjoy it – I just blasted through people! In the end I changed sport and gave football a go.

What made you leave Bristol and join Notts County?

I loved it at Bristol and it was like a family. But it was also my comfort zone and I wanted to challenge myself so I signed for Notts. Suddenly I was surrounded by international players and the standards were really high in training and in preparation for games.

But then things went really wrong for Notts County Ladies didn't they?

We didn't find out about the liquidation of the team until the morning it was announced. It didn't hit me until a few days after. Everything was being taken from you - your job, your house, your livelihood. The two months after it was announced were the worst of my life.

But then Yeovil offered you a lifeline...

Yeovil were brilliant. My confidence had gone but Yeovil felt like Bristol - a family environment. A lot of the girls there played for Wales so on the one hand, it was ideal to keep playing with them but on the other, it was feeling like I was back in my comfort zone.

And now you're at Everton...

I signed for Everton to challenge myself again. I believe we can compete in WSL1 and I am really excited to see what we can do.

And in your first season you were named the Player of the Year!

I didn't expect it! It was a great first season, the fact we turned full-time and I settled in well. The girls are amazing and the facilities we get to use are brilliant. It was a season for us to get used to WSL1 and we are all determined to keep getting better as we know we can mix it with the best teams.

THE RICHARLISON STORY

Brazilian striker Richarlison joined Everton in the summer of 2018. This is his story so far...

Q DID YOU ALWAYS PLAY FOOTBALL AS A CHILD?

I would play football whenever possible. Sometimes I'd work to help out at home. I remember selling ice lollies, home-made sweets and, occasionally, I'd work at the car wash to earn cash to buy things for the house.

Everything began at my auntie's when they put me into a football academy. I remember I had no trainers to play in so I went barefoot, while everyone else was in trainers.

It was tough but worth it, it means that today we value things more. I also remember running 9km with ripped trainers to get to training one day. The sock kept coming out of the shoe, so I'd have to stop and tuck it in.

Q YOU TRAINED WITH A BRAZILIAN TEAM CALLED FIGUEIRENSE BUT GOT RELEASED AT 17 - WAS THAT HARD TO TAKE?

I was released on my 17th birthday by Figueirense. I was really upset at the time, it ruined my birthday. I was sent home. I remember getting the flight to Victoria, the state capital and had to wait more than 10 hours at the bus station in the cold and rain. My coach told me not to give up as I was still very young. I continued working hard, rain or shine, working towards my dream.

Q THEN YOU HAD A TRIAL WITH AMERICA MINEIRO...

My dad only had enough money for the one-way bus ticket and some spare change for food, so I went without enough money to get back. I bought some food because I was hungry on the journey and I arrived intent on succeeding. I put everything into the training and was signed after two sessions. It was pure happiness and I can only thank God. It was a wonderful year for me because it was the year I achieved my goal of buying a house for my dad.

Q FLUMINENSE IS A BIG CLUB IN BRAZIL SO IT WAS A BIG MOVE TO JOIN THEM IN 2015

I was called up to the Brazil Under-20 team when I started playing regularly at Fluminense. The Professor, Abel Braga (the then Fluminense manager) gave me the opportunity. I got some momentum, nailed down my place in the team and scored a lot of goals to bring joy to the Fluminense fans.

Q HOW BIG A DECISION WAS IT TO COME TO ENGLAND AND SIGN FOR WATFORD?

It was a unique opportunity and I didn't have to think twice. It was difficult when the cold came, I wasn't used to temperatures of minus five and the snow was a bit tough for me! In terms of food, I found a Brazilian supermarket with the rice, beans and meat that I like which was helpful. It wasn't too hard to settle and I was able to quickly adapt to the country.

Q AND NOW YOU'RE AT EVERTON!

There is a great atmosphere at Goodison Park. The fans drive the team on against the opposition. It's exciting to be here as Everton have a lot of top players. I'll grow here together with my teammates and give my best every day to become a great player.

Q ARE YOU STILL CLOSE TO YOUR HOMETOWN OF NOVA VENECIA IN BRAZIL

My town is proud of me. Not just my family but everybody, I'm always well-received by everyone. Whenever I'm on holiday or have any time off, I go straight home because I'm made so welcome. I'm grateful to all those from the town who helped me. I organised a festive charity football match and we collected three tons of food which we distributed in the deprived areas of my town to bring some joy to the local kids.

GUESS MY OPPONENT!

WITH TOM DAVIES

Hi everyone,

Last season I played against many great players in the Premier League. See if you can guess who my opponent is in each of these photographs... every single one of them is an international and I'll give you an extra point if you can also tell me which country each one plays for. Good luck and thanks for all your support!

1.

2.

3.

4.

5.

6.

7.

8.

9.

10.

Answers on p61.

IDRISSA GUEYE

NAME THE MASCOT...

How much attention do you pay on a match-day?

There's always loads going on before a big Premier League game with pre-match entertainment all the way up to the kick-off.

A big part of it all are the club mascots. Here's ten Premier League mascots... which teams are they from?

Answers on p

MEET THE UNDER-23s

Here are the boys who will be playing for Everton Under-23s this season in Premier League 2...

They play their home games at Goodison Park or at Southport FC – check out evertonfc.com for the fixture list and pop along to see them in action.

JOE HILTON
Goalkeeper
Born: 11/10/99, Birkenhead

MATEUSZ HEWELT
Goalkeeper
Born: 23/09/96, Poland

TYIAS BROWNING
Defender
Born: 27/05/94, Liverpool

LEWIS GIBSON
Defender
Born: 19/07/2000, County Durham

NATHANGELO MARKELO
Defender
Born: 07/01/99, Holland

MORGAN FEENEY
Defender
Born: 08/02/99, Liverpool

DANNY BRAMALL
Defender
Born: 03/09/98, Chesterfield

ALEX DENNY
Defender
Born: 12/04/2000, Macclesfield

ANTONY EVANS
Midfielder
Born: 23/09/98, Liverpool

HARRY CHARSLEY
Midfielder
Born: 01/11/96, Wirral

DENNIS ADENIRAN
Midfielder
Born: 02/01/99, London

FRASER HORNBY
Striker
Born: 13/09/99, Northampton

MATTHEW FOULDS
Defender
Born: 17/02/98, Bradford

NATHAN BROADHEAD
Striker
Born: 05/04/98, Bangor, North Wales

JOSH BOWLER
Striker
Born: 05/03/99, London

ANTHONY GORDON
Striker
Born: 24/02/2001, Liverpool

SHANE LAVERY
Striker
Born: 08/12/98, Northern Ireland

BASSALA SAMBOU
Striker
Born: 15/10/97, Germany

CON OUZOUNIDIS
Defender
Born: 08/10/99, Australia

INSIDE FINCH FARM

Everton Football Club moved into our Finch Farm training base in October 2007. Since then, there have been a number of changes to the complex to make sure that it is still one of the best in the Premier League. Here's a sneak preview of the facility...

The main entrance.

This is the media theatre where Marco Silva does his weekly pre-match press conference.

The indoor gymnasium that gets used when the weather is really bad outside!

The players need to be at peak fitness for every game, so it's just as well the gym is well stocked with the latest equipment.

The first-team dressing room.

This is where the first-team squad chill out after training.

One of the many pitches at the complex.

The boot room.

NAME THE BOSS

Have a look these old photographs and see how many of them you can recognise!

They are all famous footy managers but these shots were taken when they were players - some of them a long time ago!

1.

2.

3.

4.

5.

6.

7.

8.

9.

10.

Answers on p61.

GROWN-UP QUIZ...

Here's a quiz for you to do with a grown-up or maybe you can be the one asking the questions!

1. Theo Walcott began his professional career at which club?

2. From which club did Everton sign Tim Cahill in 2004?

3. Which one of these former Everton players NEVER won an FA Cup final with the Blues – Kevin Sheedy, Adrian Heath or Kevin Richardson?

4. In what year did Walter Smith become Everton manager?

5. Who scored the most goals for Everton – Leon Osman or Kevin Campbell?

6. Name the four players who have played for Everton and Nigeria?

7. Last season, Wayne Rooney scored a hat–trick in a 4–0 win against West Ham, but can you remember who scored Everton's other goal that night?

8. Which team beat Everton on penalties in the FA Cup 3rd round in 2015?

9. Can you name the three Academy players who came on as substitutes to make their senior debuts at Apollon Limassol in the Europa League last season?

10. With regards to Everton, what have Arsenal defender Shkodran Mustafi and Wolves goalie John Ruddy got in common?

11. Who joined Everton on loan from LA Galaxy in January 2010?

12. Which player won 93 caps for his country while he was at Everton?

Answers on p61.

QUIZ ANSWERS

PAGE 10: HOW MUCH DO YOU KNOW ABOUT... EVERTON!

THE STADIUM – 1. 1892 2. The Bullens Road 3. b. 78,299 v Liverpool in 1948 4. True – West Germany v Russia in 1966

GOALS – 1. Oumar Niasse v West Ham 2. 60 3. Wayne Rooney 4. 7-1

PLAYERS – 1. Swansea City and Tottenham Hotspur 2. Jordan Pickford, Idrissa Gueye and Gylfi Sigurdsson 3. Yerry Mina 4. Phil Jagielka and Dominic Calvert-Lewin

LEIGHTON BAINES – 1. Wigan Athletic 2. b. Moldova 3. 30 4. Chelsea

THE FA CUP – 1. Manchester United 2. Five 3. 2009 4. a. Neville Southall

PAGE 19: CELEBRITY EVERTONIANS

1. Tommy Fleetwood 2. Amanda Holden 3. John Parrott 4. Tony Bellew 5. Liz McClarnon 6. Matt Dawson 7. Sylvester Stallone

PAGE 20: EVERTON WORDSERCH

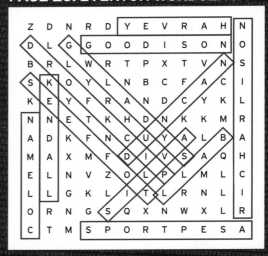

PAGE 32: SPOT THE DIFFERENCE

PAGE 33: HOME, AWAY OR DRAW!

	Home		Away	Result
1	Victor Anichebe (25)	v	Steve Pienaar (24)	H
2	Marouane Fellaini (33)	v	David Unsworth (40)	A
3	Louis Saha (35)	v	Yakubu (33)	H
4	Tomasz Radzinski (26)	v	Andy Johnson (22)	H
5	Kevin Campbell (51)	v	Tim Cahill (68)	A
6	Tony Hibbert (0)	v	Tim Howard (1)	A
7	Gerard Deulofeu (8)	v	Samuel Eto'o (4)	H
8	Sylvain Distin (5)	v	John Heitinga (5)	D
9	Thomas Gravesen (12)	v	Arouna Kone (10)	H
10	James McFadden (18)	v	Nikica Jelavic (21)	A

PAGE 41: WORLD CUP QUIZ
1. Belgium 2. Six 3. John Stones
4. Jordan Henderson 5. Belgium
6. Red cards! 7. Bottom 8. Didier
Deschamps

PAGE 45: NAME THE KEEPER
1. Hugo Lloris, Tottenham 2. David de
Gea, Manchester United
3. Kasper Schmeichel, Leicester City
4. Ederson, Manchester City
5. Kepa Arrizabalaga, Chelsea
6. Petr Cech, Arsenal 7. Nick Pope,
Burnley 8. Heurelho Gomes, Watford
9. Alex McCarthy, Southampton
10. Wayne Hennessy, Crystal Palace

PAGES 50-51: TOM DAVIES: GUESS
MY OPPONENT
1. Kevin De Bruyne, Belgium
2. N'Golo Kante, France 3. Phil
Jones, England 4. Willian, Brazil
5. Manuel Lanzini, Argentina
6. Nemanja Matic, Serbia 7. David
Silva, Spain 8. Georginio Wijnaldum,
Holland 9. Hector Bellerin, Spain
10. Andros Townsend, England

PAGE 53: NAME THE MASCOT
1. West Ham 2. Crystal Palace
3. Manchester City 4. Tottenham
Hotspur 5. Brighton & Hove Albion
6. Manchester United 7. Burnley
8. Huddersfield Town 9. Leicester
City 10. Watford

PAGE 58: NAME THE BOSS
1. Chris Hughton 2. Gareth
Southgate 3. Steve Bruce 4. Mark
Hughes 5. Pep Guardiola 6. Manuel
Pellegrini 7. Roy Hodgson 8. Martin
O'Neill 9. Didier Deschamps
10. Mauricio Pochettino

PAGE 59: GROWN-UP QUIZ...
1. Southampton 2. Millwall 3. Kevin
Sheedy 4. 1998 5. Leon Osman
6. Joseph Yobo, Yakubu, Victor
Anichebe and Daniel Amokachi
7. Ashley Williams 8. West Ham
9. Anthony Gordon, Nathan
Broadhead and Alex Denny 10. They
only made one first team appearance
for Everton 11. Landon Donovan
12. Tim Howard for the USA.